This Bucket List Journal belongs to

_____

If lost, please contact

_____

There is a
fountain of youth:
it is your mind,
your talents,
the creativity you bring
to your life
and the lives of
people you love.

- Sophia Loren

Welcome to Retirement!

Brainstorming Prompts

What is your mental picture of an ideal retirement?
What is something you have always wanted to try?
What experiences or activities in your life do you
look back on and wish you could do again?

Bucket List Brainstorming

Use the categories on the following pages to spark
ideas for the next chapter in your life. Think about
how you can combine categories, for example,
training for a walking or running race in order to
raise funds for charity.

Allow Yourself to Dream Big

Even if you can't retire to a tropical island, thinking
about what draws you to that lifestyle can help you
find some more realistic alternatives.

Less is More

Consider your current commitments and
responsabilities. What would you like to do more of
in retirement? What activities would you like to
phase out or do less of?

BUCKET LIST
LIST
BRAINSTORM

WHAT IDEAS COME TO MIND WHEN YOU THINK ABOUT YOUR RETIREMENT LIFESTYLE?

FAMILY

LEGACY

SPIRITUAL

SOCIAL CONNECTIONS

OUTDOORS

TRAVEL

CULTURE

LEARNING

CREATIVE ENDEAVORS	VOLUNTEERING	WHAT PUTS A SMILE ON YOUR FACE? WHAT ARE YOU MOST EXCITED ABOUT?
SKILLS TO DEVELOP	NEW SKILLS	ONCE IN A LIFETIME EXPERIENCES
SOLO ADVENTURES	LONGEVITY PLAN	SEASONAL BUCKET LIST ITEMS

Bucket List Item ....

I want to do this because...

....
....
....
....
....
....
....

What do I need to do to make this happen?

....
....
....
....
....
....

Date completed ....

Where ....

Do it again?   YES ☐   NO ☐

Only if ....

Memories & Reflections

....
....
....
....
....
....
....
....

Bucket List Item ....

I want to do this because...

....
....
....
....
....
....
....

What do I need to do to make this happen?

....
....
....
....
....
....
....

Date completed ....   Where ....

Do it again?   YES ☐   NO ☐   Only if ....

Memories & Reflections

....
....
....
....
....
....
....
....

Bucket List Item ....

I want to do this because...

....
....
....
....
....
....
....

What do I need to do to make this happen?

....
....
....
....
....
....
....

Date completed ....   Where ....

Do it again?   YES ☐   NO ☐   Only if ....

Memories & Reflections

....
....
....
....
....
....
....
....

Bucket List Item ....

I want to do this because...

....
....
....
....
....
....
....

What do I need to do to make this happen?

....
....
....
....
....
....
....

Date completed .... Where ....

Do it again?   YES ☐   NO ☐   Only if ....

Memories & Reflections

....
....
....
....
....
....
....
....

Bucket List Item ....

I want to do this because...

....

....

....

....

....

....

....

What do I need to do to make this happen?

....

....

....

....

....

....

....

Date completed ....

Do it again?　YES ☐　NO ☐

Where ....

Only if ....

Memories & Reflections

....

....

....

....

....

....

....

....

Bucket List Item ....

I want to do this because...

....
....
....
....
....
....
....

What do I need to do to make this happen?

....
....
....
....
....
....
....

Date completed ....   Where ....

Do it again?   YES ☐   NO ☐   Only if ....

Memories & Reflections

....
....
....
....
....
....
....
....

Bucket List Item ....

I want to do this because...

....
....
....
....
....
....
....

What do I need to do to make this happen?

....
....
....
....
....
....
....

Date completed ....   Where ....

Do it again?   YES ☐   NO ☐   Only if ....

Memories & Reflections

....
....
....
....
....
....
....
....

Bucket List Item ....

I want to do this because...

What do I need to do to make this happen?

....

....

....

....

....

....

....

Date completed ....   Where ....

Do it again? YES ☐ NO ☐   Only if ....

Memories & Reflections

....

....

....

....

....

....

....

....

Bucket List Item ....

I want to do this because...

What do I need to do to make this happen?

....
....
....
....
....
....
....

....
....
....
....
....
....
....

Date completed ....   Where ....

Do it again?   YES ☐   NO ☐   Only if ....

Memories & Reflections

....
....
....
....
....
....
....
....

Bucket List Item ....

I want to do this because...

What do I need to do to make this happen?

....
....
....
....
....
....
....

Date completed ....   Where ....

Do it again?   YES ☐   NO ☐   Only if ....

Memories & Reflections

....
....
....
....
....
....
....
....

Bucket List Item ....

I want to do this because...

....
....
....
....
....
....
....

What do I need to do to make this happen?

....
....
....
....
....
....
....

Date completed ....   Where ....

Do it again?   YES ☐   NO ☐   Only if ....

Memories & Reflections

....
....
....
....
....
....
....

Bucket List Item ....

I want to do this because...

What do I need to do to make this happen?

....

....

....

....

....

....

....

Date completed .... Where ....

Do it again?   YES ☐   NO ☐   Only if ....

Memories & Reflections

....

....

....

....

....

....

....

....

Bucket List Item ....

I want to do this because...

....
....
....
....
....
....
....

What do I need to do to make this happen?

....
....
....
....
....
....
....

Date completed ....

Do it again?   YES ☐   NO ☐

Where ....

Only if ....

Memories & Reflections

....
....
....
....
....
....
....
....

Bucket List Item ....

I want to do this because...

....
....
....
....
....
....
....

What do I need to do to make this happen?

....
....
....
....
....
....
....

Date completed ....

Do it again?   YES ☐   NO ☐

Where ....

Only if ....

Memories & Reflections

....
....
....
....
....
....
....
....

Bucket List Item ....

I want to do this because...

....
....
....
....
....
....
....

What do I need to do to make this happen?

....
....
....
....
....
....
....

Date completed ....

Where ....

Do it again?   YES ☐   NO ☐

Only if ....

Memories & Reflections

....
....
....
....
....
....
....
....

Bucket List Item ....

I want to do this because...

....
....
....
....
....
....
....

What do I need to do to make this happen?

....
....
....
....
....
....
....

Date completed ....   Where ....

Do it again?   YES ☐   NO ☐   Only if ....

Memories & Reflections

....
....
....
....
....
....
....
....

Bucket List Item ....

I want to do this because...

....
....
....
....
....
....
....

What do I need to do to make this happen?

....
....
....
....
....
....
....

Date completed ....

Where ....

Do it again?   YES ☐   NO ☐

Only if ....

Memories & Reflections

....
....
....
....
....
....
....
....

Bucket List Item ....

I want to do this because...

What do I need to do to make this happen?

....

....

....

....

....

....

....

....

....

....

....

....

....

....

Date completed ....

Where ....

Do it again?   YES ☐   NO ☐

Only if ....

Memories & Reflections

....

....

....

....

....

....

....

....

Bucket List Item ....

I want to do this because...

....
....
....
....
....
....
....

What do I need to do to make this happen?

....
....
....
....
....
....
....

Date completed ....

Do it again?   YES ☐   NO ☐

Where ....

Only if ....

Memories & Reflections

....
....
....
....
....
....
....

Bucket List Item ....

I want to do this because...

What do I need to do to make this happen?

....
....
....
....
....
....
....

....
....
....
....
....
....
....

Date completed ....   Where ....

Do it again?   YES ☐   NO ☐   Only if ....

Memories & Reflections

....
....
....
....
....
....
....
....

Bucket List Item ....

I want to do this because...

....
....
....
....
....
....
....

What do I need to do to make this happen?

....
....
....
....
....
....
....

Date completed ....   Where ....

Do it again?   YES ☐   NO ☐   Only if ....

Memories & Reflections

....
....
....
....
....
....
....
....

Bucket List Item ....

I want to do this because...

What do I need to do to make this happen?

....
....
....
....
....
....
....

Date completed ....   Where ....

Do it again?   YES ☐   NO ☐   Only if ....

Memories & Reflections

....
....
....
....
....
....
....
....

Bucket List Item ....

I want to do this because...

....
....
....
....
....
....
....

What do I need to do to make this happen?

....
....
....
....
....
....
....

Date completed ....

Where ....

Do it again?   YES ☐   NO ☐

Only if ....

Memories & Reflections

....
....
....
....
....
....
....
....

Bucket List Item ....

I want to do this because...

What do I need to do to make this happen?

....

....

....

....

....

....

....

Date completed ....   Where ....

Do it again?   YES ☐   NO ☐   Only if ....

Memories & Reflections

....

....

....

....

....

....

....

....

Bucket List Item ....

I want to do this because...

....
....
....
....
....
....
....

What do I need to do to make this happen?

....
....
....
....
....
....
....

Date completed ....

Where ....

Do it again?   YES ☐   NO ☐

Only if ....

Memories & Reflections

....
....
....
....
....
....
....
....

Bucket List Item ....

I want to do this because...

....
....
....
....
....
....
....

What do I need to do to make this happen?

....
....
....
....
....
....
....

Date completed ....

Do it again?   YES ☐   NO ☐

Where ....

Only if ....

Memories & Reflections

....
....
....
....
....
....
....
....

Bucket List Item ....

I want to do this because...

What do I need to do to make this happen?

....
....
....
....
....
....
....

....
....
....
....
....
....
....

Date completed ....

Where ....

Do it again? YES ☐ NO ☐

Only if ....

Memories & Reflections

....
....
....
....
....
....
....
....

Bucket List Item ....

I want to do this because...

....

....

....

....

....

....

....

What do I need to do to make this happen?

....

....

....

....

....

....

....

Date completed ....   Where ....

Do it again?   YES ☐   NO ☐   Only if ....

Memories & Reflections

....

....

....

....

....

....

....

....

Bucket List Item ....

I want to do this because...

....
....
....
....
....
....
....

What do I need to do to make this happen?

....
....
....
....
....
....
....

Date completed ....

Where ....

Do it again?   YES ☐   NO ☐

Only if ....

Memories & Reflections

....
....
....
....
....
....
....
....

Bucket List Item ....

I want to do this because...	What do I need to do to make this happen?
....	....
....	....
....	....
....	....
....	....
....	....
....	....

Date completed ....   Where ....

Do it again?   YES ☐   NO ☐   Only if ....

Memories & Reflections

....
....
....
....
....
....
....
....

Bucket List Item ....

I want to do this because...

....
....
....
....
....
....
....

What do I need to do to make this happen?

....
....
....
....
....
....
....

Date completed ....

Where ....

Do it again?   YES ☐   NO ☐

Only if ....

Memories & Reflections

....
....
....
....
....
....
....
....

Bucket List Item ....

I want to do this because...

....

....

....

....

....

....

....

What do I need to do to make this happen?

....

....

....

....

....

....

....

Date completed ....   Where ....

Do it again?   YES ☐   NO ☐   Only if ....

Memories & Reflections

....

....

....

....

....

....

....

....

Bucket List Item ....

I want to do this because...

....
....
....
....
....
....
....

What do I need to do to make this happen?

....
....
....
....
....
....
....

Date completed ....

Do it again?   YES ☐   NO ☐

Where ....

Only if ....

Memories & Reflections

....
....
....
....
....
....
....
....

Bucket List Item ....

I want to do this because...

....

....

....

....

....

....

....

What do I need to do to make this happen?

....

....

....

....

....

....

....

Date completed ....   Where ....

Do it again?   YES ☐   NO ☐   Only if ....

Memories & Reflections

....

....

....

....

....

....

....

....

Bucket List Item ....

I want to do this because...

What do I need to do to make this happen?

....
....
....
....
....
....
....

Date completed .... Where ....

Do it again? YES ☐   NO ☐ Only if ....

Memories & Reflections

....
....
....
....
....
....
....
....

Bucket List Item ....

I want to do this because...

....
....
....
....
....
....
....

What do I need to do to make this happen?

....
....
....
....
....
....
....

Date completed ....   Where ....

Do it again?   YES ☐   NO ☐   Only if ....

Memories & Reflections

....
....
....
....
....
....
....
....

Bucket List Item ....

I want to do this
because...

What do I need to do to
make this happen?

....
....
....
....
....
....
....

....
....
....
....
....
....
....

Date completed ....   Where ....

Do it again?   YES ☐   NO ☐   Only if ....

Memories & Reflections

....
....
....
....
....
....
....
....

Bucket List Item ....

I want to do this because...

....
....
....
....
....
....
....

What do I need to do to make this happen?

....
....
....
....
....
....
....

Date completed ....   Where ....

Do it again?   YES ☐   NO ☐   Only if ....

Memories & Reflections

....
....
....
....
....
....
....
....

Bucket List Item ....

I want to do this because...

....
....
....
....
....
....
....

What do I need to do to make this happen?

....
....
....
....
....
....
....

Date completed ....

Where ....

Do it again?   YES ☐   NO ☐

Only if ....

Memories & Reflections

....
....
....
....
....
....
....
....

Bucket List Item ....

I want to do this because...

What do I need to do to make this happen?

....
....
....
....
....
....
....

Date completed .... Where ....

Do it again?　　YES ☐　　NO ☐　　Only if ....

Memories & Reflections

....
....
....
....
....
....
....
....

Bucket List Item ....

I want to do this because...

....
....
....
....
....
....
....

What do I need to do to make this happen?

....
....
....
....
....
....
....

Date completed ....   Where ....

Do it again?   YES ☐   NO ☐   Only if ....

Memories & Reflections

....
....
....
....
....
....
....
....

Bucket List Item ....

I want to do this because...

....
....
....
....
....
....
....

What do I need to do to make this happen?

....
....
....
....
....
....
....

Date completed ....   Where ....

Do it again?   YES ☐   NO ☐   Only if ....

Memories & Reflections

....
....
....
....
....
....
....
....

Bucket List Item ....

I want to do this because...

....
....
....
....
....
....
....

What do I need to do to make this happen?

....
....
....
....
....
....
....

Date completed ....

Do it again?   YES ☐   NO ☐

Where ....

Only if ....

Memories & Reflections

....
....
....
....
....
....
....
....

Bucket List Item ....

I want to do this because...

....

....

....

....

....

....

....

What do I need to do to make this happen?

....

....

....

....

....

....

....

Date completed ....   Where ....

Do it again?   YES ☐   NO ☐   Only if ....

Memories & Reflections

....

....

....

....

....

....

....

....

Bucket List Item ....

I want to do this because...

....
....
....
....
....
....
....

What do I need to do to make this happen?

....
....
....
....
....
....
....

Date completed ....   Where ....

Do it again?   YES ☐   NO ☐   Only if ....

Memories & Reflections

....
....
....
....
....
....
....
....

Bucket List Item ....

I want to do this because...

....

....

....

....

....

....

....

What do I need to do to make this happen?

....

....

....

....

....

....

....

Date completed ....   Where ....

Do it again?   YES ☐   NO ☐   Only if ....

Memories & Reflections

....

....

....

....

....

....

....

....

Bucket List Item ....

I want to do this because...

....
....
....
....
....
....
....

What do I need to do to make this happen?

....
....
....
....
....
....
....

Date completed .... Where ....

Do it again?   YES ☐   NO ☐   Only if ....

Memories & Reflections

....
....
....
....
....
....
....
....

Bucket List Item ....

I want to do this because...

....
....
....
....
....
....
....

What do I need to do to make this happen?

....
....
....
....
....
....
....

Date completed ....   Where ....

Do it again?   YES ☐   NO ☐   Only if ....

Memories & Reflections

....
....
....
....
....
....
....
....

Bucket List Item ....

I want to do this because...

....
....
....
....
....
....
....

What do I need to do to make this happen?

....
....
....
....
....
....
....

Date completed ....

Do it again?   YES ☐   NO ☐

Where ....

Only if ....

Memories & Reflections

....
....
....
....
....
....
....
....

Bucket List Item ....

I want to do this because...

....
....
....
....
....
....
....

What do I need to do to make this happen?

....
....
....
....
....
....
....

Date completed ....   Where ....

Do it again?   YES ☐   NO ☐   Only if ....

Memories & Reflections

....
....
....
....
....
....
....
....

Bucket List Item ....

I want to do this because...

....
....
....
....
....
....
....

What do I need to do to make this happen?

....
....
....
....
....
....
....

Date completed ....

Do it again?　YES ☐　NO ☐

Where ....

Only if ....

Memories & Reflections

....
....
....
....
....
....
....
....

Bucket List Item ....

I want to do this because...

....
....
....
....
....
....
....

What do I need to do to make this happen?

....
....
....
....
....
....
....

Date completed ....   Where ....

Do it again?   YES ☐   NO ☐   Only if ....

Memories & Reflections

....
....
....
....
....
....
....
....

Bucket List Item ....

I want to do this because...

....

....

....

....

....

....

....

What do I need to do to make this happen?

....

....

....

....

....

....

....

Date completed ....   Where ....

Do it again?   YES ☐   NO ☐   Only if ....

Memories & Reflections

....

....

....

....

....

....

....

....

Bucket List Item ....

I want to do this because...

What do I need to do to make this happen?

....

....

....

....

....

....

....

Date completed ....   Where ....

Do it again?　YES ☐　NO ☐   Only if ....

Memories & Reflections

....

....

....

....

....

....

....

....

Bucket List Item ....

I want to do this because...

What do I need to do to make this happen?

....

....

....

....

....

....

....

....

....

....

....

....

....

....

Date completed .... Where ....

Do it again?   YES ☐   NO ☐   Only if ....

Memories & Reflections

....

....

....

....

....

....

....

....

Bucket List Item ....

I want to do this because...

....
....
....
....
....
....
....

What do I need to do to make this happen?

....
....
....
....
....
....
....

Date completed ....   Where ....

Do it again?   YES ☐   NO ☐   Only if ....

Memories & Reflections

....
....
....
....
....
....
....
....

Bucket List Item ....

I want to do this because...

....
....
....
....
....
....
....

What do I need to do to make this happen?

....
....
....
....
....
....
....

Date completed ....   Where ....

Do it again?   YES ☐   NO ☐   Only if ....

Memories & Reflections

....
....
....
....
....
....
....
....

Bucket List Item ....

I want to do this because...

....

....

....

....

....

....

....

What do I need to do to make this happen?

....

....

....

....

....

....

....

Date completed ....

Where ....

Do it again?   YES ☐   NO ☐

Only if ....

Memories & Reflections

....

....

....

....

....

....

....

....

Bucket List Item ....

I want to do this because...

What do I need to do to make this happen?

....
....
....
....
....
....
....

....
....
....
....
....
....
....

Date completed .... Where ....

Do it again?   YES ☐   NO ☐   Only if ....

Memories & Reflections

....
....
....
....
....
....
....
....

Bucket List Item ....

I want to do this because...

....

....

....

....

....

....

....

What do I need to do to make this happen?

....

....

....

....

....

....

Date completed ....   Where ....

Do it again?   YES ☐   NO ☐   Only if ....

Memories & Reflections

....

....

....

....

....

....

....

....

Bucket List Item ....

I want to do this because...

....
....
....
....
....
....
....

What do I need to do to make this happen?

....
....
....
....
....
....
....

Date completed ....   Where ....

Do it again?   YES ☐   NO ☐   Only if ....

Memories & Reflections

....
....
....
....
....
....
....
....

Bucket List Item ....

I want to do this because...

....

....

....

....

....

....

....

What do I need to do to make this happen?

....

....

....

....

....

....

....

Date completed ....

Where ....

Do it again?   YES ☐   NO ☐

Only if ....

Memories & Reflections

....

....

....

....

....

....

....

....

Bucket List Item ....

I want to do this because...

....

....

....

....

....

....

....

What do I need to do to make this happen?

....

....

....

....

....

....

....

Date completed ....

Where ....

Do it again?   YES ☐   NO ☐

Only if ....

Memories & Reflections

....

....

....

....

....

....

....

....

Bucket List Item ....

I want to do this because...

....
....
....
....
....
....
....

What do I need to do to make this happen?

....
....
....
....
....
....
....

Date completed ....

Do it again?   YES ☐   NO ☐

Where ....

Only if ....

Memories & Reflections

....
....
....
....
....
....
....
....

Bucket List Item ....

I want to do this because...

....
....
....
....
....
....
....

What do I need to do to make this happen?

....
....
....
....
....
....
....

Date completed ....   Where ....

Do it again?   YES ☐   NO ☐   Only if ....

Memories & Reflections

....
....
....
....
....
....
....
....

Bucket List Item ....

I want to do this because...

....
....
....
....
....
....
....

What do I need to do to make this happen?

....
....
....
....
....
....
....

Date completed ....

Where ....

Do it again?   YES ☐   NO ☐

Only if ....

Memories & Reflections

....
....
....
....
....
....
....
....

Bucket List Item ....

I want to do this because...

....
....
....
....
....
....
....

What do I need to do to make this happen?

....
....
....
....
....
....
....

Date completed ....

Where ....

Do it again?   YES ☐   NO ☐

Only if ....

Memories & Reflections

....
....
....
....
....
....
....
....

Bucket List Item ....

I want to do this because...

What do I need to do to make this happen?

....
....
....
....
....
....
....

....
....
....
....
....
....
....

Date completed ....   Where ....

Do it again?   YES ☐   NO ☐   Only if ....

Memories & Reflections

....
....
....
....
....
....
....
....

Bucket List Item ....

I want to do this because...

....
....
....
....
....
....
....

What do I need to do to make this happen?

....
....
....
....
....
....
....

Date completed ....   Where ....

Do it again?   YES ☐   NO ☐   Only if ....

Memories & Reflections

....
....
....
....
....
....
....
....

Bucket List Item ....

I want to do this because...

What do I need to do to make this happen?

....

....

....

....

....

....

....

....

....

....

....

....

....

....

Date completed ....

Where ....

Do it again?   YES ☐   NO ☐

Only if ....

Memories & Reflections

....

....

....

....

....

....

....

....

Bucket List Item ....

I want to do this because...

....
....
....
....
....
....
....

What do I need to do to make this happen?

....
....
....
....
....
....
....

Date completed ....

Where ....

Do it again?   YES ☐   NO ☐

Only if ....

Memories & Reflections

....
....
....
....
....
....
....
....

Bucket List Item ....

I want to do this because...

....
....
....
....
....
....
....

What do I need to do to make this happen?

....
....
....
....
....
....
....

Date completed ....

Where ....

Do it again?   YES ☐   NO ☐

Only if ....

Memories & Reflections

....
....
....
....
....
....
....
....

Bucket List Item ....

I want to do this because...

What do I need to do to make this happen?

....
....
....
....
....
....
....

Date completed .... Where ....

Do it again?   YES ☐   NO ☐   Only if ....

Memories & Reflections

....
....
....
....
....
....
....
....

Bucket List Item ....

I want to do this because...

....

....

....

....

....

....

....

What do I need to do to make this happen?

....

....

....

....

....

....

....

Date completed ....

Do it again?   YES ☐   NO ☐

Where ....

Only if ....

Memories & Reflections

....

....

....

....

....

....

....

....

Bucket List Item ....

I want to do this because...

....
....
....
....
....
....
....

What do I need to do to make this happen?

....
....
....
....
....
....
....

Date completed ....   Where ....

Do it again?   YES ☐   NO ☐   Only if ....

Memories & Reflections

....
....
....
....
....
....
....
....

Bucket List Item ....

I want to do this because...

....

....

....

....

....

....

....

What do I need to do to make this happen?

....

....

....

....

....

....

....

Date completed ....

Where ....

Do it again?   YES ☐   NO ☐

Only if ....

Memories & Reflections

....

....

....

....

....

....

....

....

Bucket List Item ....

I want to do this because...

....

....

....

....

....

....

....

What do I need to do to make this happen?

....

....

....

....

....

....

....

Date completed .... Where ....

Do it again?   YES ☐   NO ☐   Only if ....

Memories & Reflections

....

....

....

....

....

....

....

....

Bucket List Item ....

I want to do this because...

What do I need to do to make this happen?

....
....
....
....
....
....
....

....
....
....
....
....
....
....

Date completed ....

Where ....

Do it again?   YES ☐   NO ☐

Only if ....

Memories & Reflections

....
....
....
....
....
....
....
....

Bucket List Item

I want to do this because...

....
....
....
....
....
....
....

What do I need to do to make this happen?

....
....
....
....
....
....
....

Date completed .... Where ....

Do it again?   YES ☐   NO ☐   Only if ....

Memories & Reflections

....
....
....
....
....
....
....
....

Bucket List Item ....

I want to do this because...

What do I need to do to make this happen?

....

....

....

....

....

....

....

....

....

....

....

....

....

....

Date completed ....

Where ....

Do it again?   YES ☐   NO ☐

Only if ....

Memories & Reflections

....

....

....

....

....

....

....

....

Bucket List Item ....

I want to do this because...

What do I need to do to make this happen?

....
....
....
....
....
....
....

....
....
....
....
....
....
....

Date completed ....

Where ....

Do it again?   YES ☐   NO ☐

Only if ....

Memories & Reflections

....
....
....
....
....
....
....
....

Bucket List Item ....

I want to do this because...

....

....

....

....

....

....

....

What do I need to do to make this happen?

....

....

....

....

....

....

....

Date completed ....   Where ....

Do it again?   YES ☐   NO ☐   Only if ....

Memories & Reflections

....

....

....

....

....

....

....

....

Bucket List Item ....

I want to do this because...

What do I need to do to make this happen?

....
....
....
....
....
....
....

....
....
....
....
....
....
....

Date completed ....   Where ....

Do it again?   YES ☐   NO ☐   Only if ....

Memories & Reflections

....
....
....
....
....
....
....
....

Bucket List Item ....

I want to do this because...

....

....

....

....

....

....

....

What do I need to do to make this happen?

....

....

....

....

....

....

....

Date completed ....

Do it again?   YES ☐   NO ☐

Where ....

Only if ....

Memories & Reflections

....

....

....

....

....

....

....

....

Bucket List Item ....

I want to do this because...

....
....
....
....
....
....
....

What do I need to do to make this happen?

....
....
....
....
....
....
....

Date completed ....

Where ....

Do it again?   YES ☐   NO ☐

Only if ....

Memories & Reflections

....
....
....
....
....
....
....
....

Bucket List Item ....

I want to do this because...

....
....
....
....
....
....
....

What do I need to do to make this happen?

....
....
....
....
....
....
....

Date completed ....

Do it again?   YES ☐   NO ☐

Where ....

Only if ....

Memories & Reflections

....
....
....
....
....
....
....
....

Bucket List Item ....

I want to do this because...

....
....
....
....
....
....
....

What do I need to do to make this happen?

....
....
....
....
....
....
....

Date completed ....   Where ....

Do it again?   YES ☐   NO ☐   Only if ....

Memories & Reflections

....
....
....
....
....
....
....
....

Bucket List Item ....

I want to do this because...

....
....
....
....
....
....
....

What do I need to do to make this happen?

....
....
....
....
....
....
....

Date completed .... Where ....

Do it again?   YES ☐   NO ☐   Only if ....

Memories & Reflections

....
....
....
....
....
....
....

Bucket List Item ....

I want to do this because...

....
....
....
....
....
....
....

What do I need to do to make this happen?

....
....
....
....
....
....
....

Date completed ....   Where ....

Do it again?   YES ☐   NO ☐   Only if ....

Memories & Reflections

....
....
....
....
....
....
....
....

Bucket List Item ....

I want to do this because...

....

....

....

....

....

....

....

What do I need to do to make this happen?

....

....

....

....

....

....

....

Date completed ....   Where ....

Do it again?   YES ☐   NO ☐   Only if ....

Memories & Reflections

....

....

....

....

....

....

....

....

Bucket List Item ....

I want to do this because...

....
....
....
....
....
....
....

What do I need to do to make this happen?

....
....
....
....
....
....
....

Date completed ....   Where ....

Do it again?   YES ☐   NO ☐   Only if ....

Memories & Reflections

....
....
....
....
....
....
....
....

Bucket List Item ....

I want to do this because...

....
....
....
....
....
....
....

What do I need to do to make this happen?

....
....
....
....
....
....
....

Date completed ....   Where ....

Do it again?   YES ☐   NO ☐   Only if ....

Memories & Reflections

....
....
....
....
....
....
....
....

Bucket List Item

I want to do this because...

....

....

....

....

....

....

....

What do I need to do to make this happen?

....

....

....

....

....

....

....

Date completed ....

Do it again?   YES ☐   NO ☐

Where ....

Only if ....

Memories & Reflections

....

....

....

....

....

....

....

....

Bucket List Item ....

I want to do this because...

....

....

....

....

....

....

....

What do I need to do to make this happen?

....

....

....

....

....

....

....

Date completed ....   Where ....

Do it again?   YES ☐   NO ☐   Only if ....

Memories & Reflections

....

....

....

....

....

....

....

....

Bucket List Item ....

I want to do this because...

....

....

....

....

....

....

....

What do I need to do to make this happen?

....

....

....

....

....

....

....

Date completed .... Where ....

Do it again?   YES ☐   NO ☐   Only if ....

Memories & Reflections

....

....

....

....

....

....

....

....

Bucket List Item ....

I want to do this because...

What do I need to do to make this happen?

....

....

....

....

....

....

....

Date completed ....   Where ....

Do it again?   YES ☐   NO ☐   Only if ....

Memories & Reflections

....

....

....

....

....

....

....

....

Bucket List Item ....

I want to do this because...

....

....

....

....

....

....

....

What do I need to do to make this happen?

....

....

....

....

....

....

....

Date completed ....

Where ....

Do it again?   YES ☐   NO ☐

Only if ....

Memories & Reflections

....

....

....

....

....

....

....

....

Bucket List Item ....

I want to do this because...

What do I need to do to make this happen?

....
....
....
....
....
....
....

....
....
....
....
....
....
....

Date completed ....

Where ....

Do it again?   YES ☐   NO ☐

Only if ....

Memories & Reflections

....
....
....
....
....
....
....
....

Bucket List Item ....

I want to do this because...

....
....
....
....
....
....
....

What do I need to do to make this happen?

....
....
....
....
....
....
....

Date completed ....   Where ....

Do it again?   YES ☐   NO ☐   Only if ....

Memories & Reflections

....
....
....
....
....
....
....
....

Bucket List Item ....

I want to do this because...

....

....

....

....

....

....

....

What do I need to do to make this happen?

....

....

....

....

....

....

....

Date completed ....

Where ....

Do it again?   YES ☐   NO ☐

Only if ....

Memories & Reflections

....

....

....

....

....

....

....

....

Bucket List Item ....

I want to do this because...

....
....
....
....
....
....
....

What do I need to do to make this happen?

....
....
....
....
....
....
....

Date completed ....   Where ....

Do it again?   YES ☐   NO ☐   Only if ....

Memories & Reflections

....
....
....
....
....
....
....
....

Bucket List Item ....

I want to do this because...

....

....

....

....

....

....

....

What do I need to do to make this happen?

....

....

....

....

....

....

....

Date completed ....

Do it again?   YES ☐   NO ☐

Where ....

Only if ....

Memories & Reflections

....

....

....

....

....

....

....

....

Bucket List Item ....

I want to do this because...

....
....
....
....
....
....
....

What do I need to do to make this happen?

....
....
....
....
....
....
....

Date completed ....   Where ....

Do it again?   YES ☐   NO ☐   Only if ....

Memories & Reflections

....
....
....
....
....
....
....
....

Bucket List Item ....

I want to do this because...

....

....

....

....

....

....

....

What do I need to do to make this happen?

....

....

....

....

....

....

....

Date completed ....   Where ....

Do it again?   YES ☐   NO ☐   Only if ....

Memories & Reflections

....

....

....

....

....

....

....

....

Bucket List Item ....

I want to do this because...

....
....
....
....
....
....
....

What do I need to do to make this happen?

....
....
....
....
....
....
....

Date completed ....   Where ....

Do it again?   YES ☐   NO ☐   Only if ....

Memories & Reflections

....
....
....
....
....
....
....
....

Made in the USA
Middletown, DE
15 June 2023

32655231R00062